Alpha Beta Chowder

ALPHA BETA CHOWDER

by Jeanne Steig
Pictures by William Steig

Michael di Capua Books

HarperCollins

For my sisters,
Sue, Lisa, and Cathy

FOREWORD

A chowder is a robust goop
That's more akin to stew than soup.
It can be brackish or divine.
Sit down and take a taste of mine.

An Appetizer for Alexander

Abhorent axolotl, scat!
Unless you'd like to feed my cat.

Come at once, dear Alexander,
Have a bit of salamander.
See its tasty little gills?
Don't they look like lamb-chop frills?

Amphibian, avoid thy fate.
Slither off! Absquatulate!

Bellicose Brigand vs. Belligerent Bear

A bear and a brigand were bickering bitterly
Under the shade of a baobab tree.
"The best thing by far," bawled the brigand, "is baklava."
"Bosh!" boomed the bear. "It can't possibly be.

"Why, there's bric-a-brac, ipecac, blubber, and broccoli,
Bamboo, banana oil, beetles, and brine."
"You bandy-legged brute," brayed the brigand, "you blatherskite!
Baklava beats them all any old time."

Oh, what a brouhaha: "Baklava!" "Balderdash!"
"Bah!" barked the bear. "We shall never agree."
"Let us pause," breathed the brigand, "and banish this blabber with
Hot buttered bat bread and barnacle tea."

Coaxing Carrotina

Come on, Cousin Carrotina,
Do pick up your concertina!
Play again that shrill cadenza,
Though it split the old credenza,
Though the cat broke out in blisters,
Though it mortifies your sisters
(If they want their music mellow,
Let them learn to play the cello),
Though it gave the goose consumption—
That cadenza sure has gumption!

Adorable Daphne, Deplorable Dora

Doesn't Daphne dress divinely?
Not like Dora, drab and dreary.
Daphne's dreamy draped in damask
(Even when her lipstick's smeary).

Dora in that dismal dirndl,
Dim and droopy—most distressing.
And that doodad like a doily
On her head—oh, how depressing.

No denying Daphne's dazzling,
With her devastating dimples.
Dora's definitely dowdy
(What a shame, about those pimples).

Dizzy Daphne, such a darling.
Dora, dull beyond repairing.
How distasteful to declare it:
One's a mermaid, one's a herring.

The Enigmatic Egg

The egg is seamless, white or brown.
It takes an oval form.
If you should find one in your path,
And if it should be warm,
Encourage it, spare no expense
Of effort, time, or care,
But gently, earnestly enquire,
"Is anybody there?"
The egg, emboldened, may erupt.
Take heed! Don't touch the thing.
For heaven knows what waits inside,
Or whether it will sting.

Feckless Father's Foolish Frolic

Friday, Father, feeling frisky,
Flew to fabled Bora Bora.
There, though warned that it was risky,
Father doffed his felt fedora.

Father, Father, oh, what folly!
Fierce the sun of Bora Bora!
Nonetheless, you *did* look jolly,
All festooned in native flora.

My Gruesome Gilbert

Gilbert's such a greedy glutton
When he gnaws a leg of mutton.
All his garments are so greasy
They would make a gibbon queasy,
And his teeth are green and gooey,
Oh, so gorgeously mildewy!

Gilbert smells like old galoshes
(Grandma swears he never washes).
Gilbert's generally vastly,
Grandly, gallopingly ghastly.
No, he isn't worth one filbert,
But I'm gaga over Gilbert.

The Heebie-jeebies

A harpy had the hiccups,
She had lumbago, too.
"Some hag," squawked she, "is hexing me,
But I know what to do.

"I'll hurl my hocus-pocus
Upon her horrid head.
I'll make her itch and howl and twitch
And wish that she was dead."

The harpy hopped and hoodooed.
The hag, she whooped and cried.
She scratched and squealed, she lurched and reeled,
And hunkered down and died.

Intolerance

Iggledy-piggledy
Ivan the Terrible
Said, "I'm inclined to be
Irksome, it's true.

"Anything triggers my
Irascibility—
Infants, for instance,
Or gum on my shoe."

Jamboree

Just be patient, Jasper Jack,
You shall have your jam jar back.
Janet took it for a joke.
Lucky thing it isn't broke.

Janet juggles very well.
Funny, how that jam jar fell.
Jealous Jason jostled Jan,
Made her drop her frying pan,

Made her drop the jellyfish—
What a jughead Jason is!
Here's your jar. Some jam remains.
Thank poor Janet for her pains.

King Kang

Ken, the killer kangaroo,
Knows karate, plays kazoo,
Knits his keeper khaki kilts,
Clowns around on lacquered stilts.
Cockeyed, knock-kneed Kenny's quick.
If you cross him,

       Ken

          can

             kick!

Lovey Dovey

A lunatic living in Lvov
Looked long at a lone turtledove.
"Though limp and lackluster,
She's no feather duster,"
Crowed he. "La-di-da, I'm in love!"

Mishmash

Making mashed potatoes, Myron?
Must you mix them with the hammer?
This bizarre, misguided method
Causes quite a katzenjammer.

Might you add the milk and butter
In a more majestic manner?
Might a mallet not be better?
That would minimize the clamor.

Noisome Naomi

"Naomi's such a nuisance,"
  The neighbors all complain.
"That nasty little numbskull,
  She's at it once again.

"Her voice is like a needle,
  Her tales are never true.
  Her language is so noxious
  It turns the devil blue!

"Naomi is a nightmare,
  She's nervy as a newt.
  Her ma and pa are nitwits—
  They think Naomi's cute."

Obadiah Overcome

Obadiah, feeling offish,
Said, "It must have been those crawfish.
Oftentimes an old crustacean
Causes inner consternation.
It'll kill you, if you let it.
I ought never to have et it.
All the same," groaned Obadiah,
"I enjoyed that jambalaya."

A Pianist Plummets

Penelope, provoking child,
How pointless and ill-bred
To plunge from your piano stool,
Pretending to be dead.

It puts poor Mother into fits,
It causes Papa pain;
And presently you must arise
To play your scales again.

Quentin Quails

Quick-witted Quentin rode out on a quest
With a quill in his hat and a quaint quilted vest.
He was flung into quicksand, got caught in a squall,
Squirmed out of a quagmire, an earthquake, a brawl.
He acquired, for his trouble, the hand of the Queen—
Quite a quarrelsome creature. And squint-eyed. And mean.

When Real Men Rode the Range

A rancher roped a rustler
And dragged him to his ranch.
He hanged that ring-tailed rattler
From a rotten redwood branch.

The branch broke off abruptly.
The rascal raced away.
"That reptile!" raged the rancher.
"I'll roast his ribs someday!"

The rogue went right on rustling.
"Goldarn!" the rancher said.
"I'll nab that mangy rodent
And pump him full of lead."

He bagged him down in Rawhide.
The pair stood chin to chin.
"Repent, you old rapscallion!
I'm here to claim your skin!"

The renegade roared, "Polecat!
It ain't no use to yell.
Your rootin'-tootin' carcass
Is on its way to hell!"

They raised an awful ruckus,
Shed fourteen quarts of blood.
"Tarnation!" rasped the roughneck.
And then he hit the mud.

"I never should have rustled,
  Or drank or smoked or swore.
  Farewell, rip-roaring rancher.
  My reckless life is o'er.

"Remember me to Mother,
  Unsaddle my poor roan.
  Inscribe these words above me
  Upon a simple stone:

"'Here lies a worthless varmint.
  Hark to his wretched tale!
  He missed the Road to Glory
  And took the Devil's Trail.'"

Shipwrecked Sailors Salvage Stilton

A ship named *Shirley* struck a shoal.
Her sailors sang a hymn.
The *Shirley* split and down she sank.
The seamen couldn't swim.

The skipper and a stowaway
Survived to splash ashore,
Where they lay sprawled upon the strand
And swore they'd sail no more:

"We'll squelch the sand between our toes
And scorn the seething seas—
A pair of shiftless so-and-sos
With sixty tons of cheese."

Toby Twits Tina

Toby's teasing can be tasteless—
Taunting, tweaking tiny Tina.
Tadpoles in her tapioca!
Thumbtacks in her semolina!

Toby ought to be more tactful.
If he's tempted to torment her,
Let him tickle, *never* throttle,
Never thump her, lest he dent her.

An Unlikely Union

My uncle comes from Utah,
Aunt Eunice comes from Mars.
They met in Ursa Major,
Adrift among the stars.

My uncle acted rashly,
He hailed a U.F.O.
It made an urgent U-turn
And hooked him by the toe.

Aunt Eunice hung from Uncle,
They traveled upside down.
They landed in the U.S.A.—
In Uncle's own hometown!

The universe is everywhere,
The universe is deep.
Aunt Eunice makes unearthly noise
Whenever she's asleep.

A Verse to Vera

Vera's vanished overnight,
Leaving her valise behind her.
Isn't Vera impolite!
Or did evil fortune find her?

Has she vaporized, alas?
Has a vampire's venom downed her?
Something vile has come to pass.
Where's that vexing girl, confound her!

Worrywart

"Whatever happened to your waist!"
  The warthog's wife exclaimed.
"How weirdly wide you have become!
  Why aren't you ashamed?"

"Ah, woe is me," the warthog wailed,
"My wardrobe doesn't fit.
  I've gained such wobbly wads of weight,
  My woolen pants are split.

"I waddle wildly when I walk,
  And weep to contemplate
  How winningly I used to waltz.
  My polka was first-rate."

"When we," his wife went on, "were wed,
  You were a winsome lad,
  While now you are a wheezing wreck!
  It's worrisome and sad."

  The warthog wrung his heavy hooves.
"Dear Wife, I'm mortified.
  I'll whittle down this wretched flesh—
  I give my word," he cried.

"I'll live on watercress and weeds
  Till I am willow thin.
  And you and I shall waltz once more.
  Next Wednesday I begin!"

Exegesis on the Sphinx

Xavier Max, that explorer of note,
Went to view the Great Sphinx. He remarked (and I quote):
"This beast has attained an exorbitant size.
It's excessive in torso but thin in the thighs.
In my expert opinion, it can't have been fleet—
Observe those extravagant, extra-large feet!
I expect it relaxed here to have a good think.
Exhausted, it slept—and awakened extinct."

Yakety Yak

" 'Twas a year ago yesterday," yammered the yak,
"That a youth with a yataghan jumped on my back.
'To Yonkers!' cried he, as he flourished his sword,
'To Yonkers at once, I'm atrociously bored!'

"Well, I shrugged him off smartly. 'You yahoo,' I said,
'You must have been born with a yam for a head.
Had you yearned for the Yukon, I might have concurred.
But July down in Yonkers…' (I yawned.) 'How absurd.'"

Blizzard Zaps Zelda

Zelda's fire has fizzled out.
She will freeze to death, no doubt.
Listen to her sniff and sneeze.
Zelda, zip your parka.

Please.